SMART ABOUT SPORTS

Meet the
Red Sox

By
Mike Kennedy
with Mark Stewart

NORWOODHOUSEPRESS

Norwood House Press, P.O. Box 316598, Chicago, Illinois 60631

For information regarding Norwood House Press,
please visit our website at: www.norwoodhousepress.com or call 866-565-2900.

Photo Credits:
   Getty Images (1, 4, 7, 8, 22), Sportschrome (15, 20, 21, 23 left), Icon SMI (12, 13), Associated Press (16),
   Black Book Partners (18).
Cover Photos:
   Top Left: Topps, Inc.; Top Right: Associated Press, Bottom Left: Jim McIsaac/Getty Images; Bottom Right: Topps, Inc.
The baseball memorabilia photographed for this book is part of the authors' collection:
   Page 6) Tris Speaker Card: Cracker Jack/F.W. Ruckhcim & Brother.   Page 10) Tris Speaker Card: Recruit Little Cigars;
   Carl Yastrzemski Card: Topps, Inc.; Carlton Fisk Card: Hostess Twinkies/Interstate Bakeries Corporation; Ted Williams
   Pin: Topps, Inc.   Page 11) Jim Rice Card: Topps, Inc.; Wade Boggs Card: Fleer Corporation; Pedro Martinez Card:
   Topps, Inc.; Nomar Garciaparra Card: The Upper Deck Company.
Special thanks to Topps, Inc.

Editor: Brian Fitzgerald
Designer: Ron Jaffe
Project Management: Black Book Partners, LLC.
Editorial Production: Jessica McCulloch

LIBRARY OF CONGRESS CATALOGING-IN-PUBLICATION DATA
      Kennedy, Mike (Mike William), 1965-
      Meet the Red Sox / by Mike Kennedy with Mark Stewart.
         p. cm. -- (Smart about sports)
      Includes bibliographical references and index.
      Summary: "An introductory look at the Boston Red Sox baseball team.
   Includes a brief history, facts, photos, records, glossary, and fun
   activities"--Provided by publisher.
      ISBN-13: 978-1-59953-368-1 (library edition : alk. paper)
      ISBN-10: 1-59953-368-5 (library edition : alk. paper)
      1. Boston Red Sox (Baseball team)--Juvenile literature. I. Stewart, Mark,
   1960- II. Title.
      GV875.B62K456 2010
      796.357'64'0974461--dc22
                              2009042927

Manufactured in the United States of America in North Mankato, Minnesota.
N147—012010

Contents

Words in **bold type** are defined on page 24.

Jonathan Papelbon celebrates with Jason Varitek after Boston's 2007 World Series championship.

The Boston Red Sox

If you could pick the name of a sports team, what would it be? Would you choose a scary name like Tigers or Sharks? Many years ago, the Boston baseball team was named after the color of its socks. The Red Sox do not have a scary name, but they can be a scary team to play.

Once Upon a Time

The Red Sox played their first season in 1901. They were part of a new league called the American League (AL). More than 100 years have passed since then.

The Red Sox have always put great players on the field. Their famous hitters include

SPEAKER, Boston - Americans

Tris Speaker, Jimmie Foxx, Ted Williams, Jim Rice, and David Ortiz. Their famous pitchers include Cy Young, Jim Lonborg, Roger Clemens, Pedro Martinez, and Jonathan Papelbon.

Ted Williams shows off his smooth swing.

The Red Sox play a night game at Fenway Park.

At the Ballpark

The Red Sox play their home games in Fenway Park. Fenway Park is a very old stadium. It opened in 1912. The wall in left field is 37 feet tall. It was built this tall so batters would not hit too many home runs. When players stand in front of this wall, they look very small. Fans call the wall the "Green Monster."

Shoe Box

The cards and pins on these pages belong to the authors. They show some of the best Red Sox ever.

Tris Speaker

Outfielder • 1907–1915
Tris Speaker was a great hitter and fielder. In 1912, he led the league in doubles and home runs.

Carl Yastrzemski

Outfielder • 1961–1983
Everyone knew Carl Yastrzemski as "Yaz." He was the last player to win the **Triple Crown**.

Ted Williams

Outfielder • 1939–1960
Ted Williams was the last player to hit over .400 in a season. He was a batting champion six times.

Carlton Fisk

Catcher • 1969–1980
Carlton Fisk's nickname was "Pudge." He hit a famous home run during the World Series in 1975.

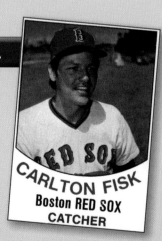

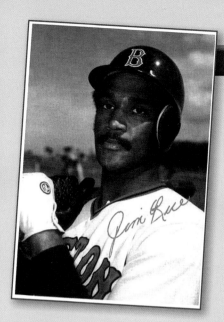

Jim Rice

Outfielder • 1974–1989
Jim Rice was a powerful hitter. Many pitchers were scared of him. No one hit a baseball harder than he did.

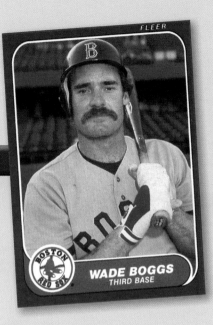

Wade Boggs

Third Baseman • 1982–1992
Wade Boggs would only eat chicken on game day. It worked, because he won five batting championships.

Nomar Garciaparra

Shortstop • 1996–2004
Nomar Garciaparra was a batting champion in 1999 and again in 2000. In 2003, he married Mia Hamm, the soccer star.

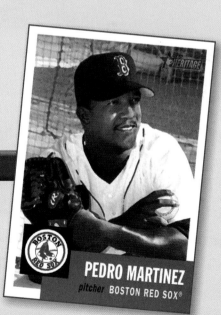

Pedro Martinez

Pitcher • 1998–2004
Pedro Martinez was a little man who pitched like a giant. He led the league in strikeouts three times.

ABC's of Baseball

In this picture of Dustin Pedroia, how many things can you find that begin with the letter **B**?

See page 23 for answer.

Brain Games

Here is a poem about a great Boston star:

There once was a hurler named Schilling.
His fastball and curveball were thrilling.
Even when he was hurt
This pitcher called Curt
Was able and ready and willing.

Guess which one of these facts is **TRUE**:

⚾ *Curt started his own video game company.*

⚾ *Curt once threw a pitch out of Fenway Park.*

See page 23 for answer.

Curt Schilling became a hero to Red Sox fans in 2004 when he pitched after having ankle surgery.

15

Wally likes to have fun with fans.

Fun on the Field

One of the first things fans see at a Red Sox game is the "Green Monster." Yes, the famous left field wall, but this is also the name of the team mascot!

Meet Wally, the Green Monster. Wally's best friend is Jerry Remy. Remy announces the team's games on TV. He has written two books about Wally: *Hello Wally* and *Wally the Green Monster and His Journey Through Red Sox Nation.*

On the Map

The Red Sox call Boston, Massachusetts home. Their players come from all over the country—and all over the world. Match these Most Valuable Players (MVPs) with the places they were born:

1 **Jimmie Foxx** • 1938 AL MVP
Sudlersville, Maryland

2 **Fred Lynn** • 1975 AL MVP
Chicago, Illinois

3 **Manny Ramirez**
2004 World Series MVP
Santo Domingo, Dominican Republic

4 **Josh Beckett** •
2007 American League
Championship Series MVP
Spring, Texas

5 **Dustin Pedroia** • 2008 AL MVP
Woodland, California

United States Map

5

2

1

4

★ The Red Sox play
in Boston, Massachusetts.

World Map

3

What's in the Locker?

Baseball teams wear different uniforms for home games and away games. Boston's home uniform is bright white. The uniform top spells out **R-E-D S-O-X** in red and blue letters.

Kevin Youkilis wears the team's home uniform.

Boston's away uniform is gray. It also has blue letters. The uniform top spells out **B-O-S-T-O-N**. At home and away, the players wear a blue cap with the letter **B** on the front.

Jacoby Ellsbury wears the team's away uniform.

21

We Won!

In the early part of the 1900s, the Red Sox had a great team. They won the World Series five times. After that, Boston could not win the World Series again. Some fans thought the Red Sox were "cursed."

In 2004, the Red Sox returned to the World Series. They beat the St. Louis Cardinals. Now fans have forgotten all about the famous curse.

Jason Varitek jumps into Keith Foulke's arms after the 2004 World Series.

Record Book

These Red Sox stars set amazing team records.

Hitter	Record	Year
Jimmie Foxx	175 **Runs Batted In**	1938
Ted Williams	.406 **Batting Average**	1941
David Ortiz	54 Home Runs	2006

Pitcher	Record	Year
Joe Wood	34 Wins	1912
Tom Gordon	46 **Saves**	1998
Pedro Martinez	313 Strikeouts	1999

Answer for ABC's of Baseball

Here are words in the picture that start with **B**:
Base, Baseline, Bat, Batter, Batting Glove, Batting Helmet,
Belt. Did you find any others?

Answer for Brain Games

The first fact is true. Curt Schilling started a video game
company called 38 Studios. He pitched for four seasons
in Boston and won 21 games in 2004.

23

Baseball Words

BATTING AVERAGE
A measure of how often a batter gets a hit. A .300 average is very good.

RUNS BATTED IN
The number of runners that score on a batter's hits and walks.

SAVES
A number that shows how many times a pitcher comes into a game and completes a win for his team.

TRIPLE CROWN
An honor given to a player who leads the league in home runs, batting average, and runs batted in.

Index

Photos are on **bold** numbered pages.

About the Red Sox

Learn more about the Red Sox at boston.redsox.mlb.com

Learn more about baseball at www.baseballhalloffame.org